My Zayde

A Recollection

My Zayde
A Recollection

By
Richard Morris Usatinsky

Illustrations by
Judith Sol-Dyess

Satin Sky Press
Chicago

Acknowledgements

Special thanks to Dr. James Fairhall, DePaul University; Dr. Albert Erlebacher, DePaul University; Abbott Chrisman; Alex Satin; Mary and Bernard Lurie; Terri Morris; Miriam Mayer; Aviva Sorkin; Cantor Phil Lind; Bina Nadler; Davis Scott; Dan Poynter

Text Copyright © 1994 by Richard Morris Usatinsky
Illustrations Copyright © 1994 by Judith Sol-Dyess

Satin Sky Press

P.O. Box 10646
Chicago, Ilinois 60610–0646

All Rights Reserved

ISBN 1–884341–00–4 (paper): $10.00
ISBN 1–884341–01–2 (cloth) : $18.00

Library of Congress Catalog Card Number 93-86375

Book design by Richard G. Smith

Printed with soy-based ink on recycled paper

Manufactured in the United States of America

1 3 5 7 9 10 8 6 4 2

Contents

Dedicated to the loving memory of one man:

Yehoshua Usatinsky
Owsiej Usiatynski
Sheika Satin
Sam Satin

my zayde
(1890–1980)

And for my family

The Fifth Candle of Chanukah

In the cold grayness
of a winter's day,
where solitude and wind part the clouds
long enough for a ray of sunlight to shine in
through the dirty window
and warm the cold, damp room —
long enough to etch a smile upon faces
where frowns are usually worn.
Sunlight.
Like the drop of oil that burned
for eight days and eight nights,
that lit the temple
and branded life and salvation upon the
souls of the Macabees.
Behold, a miracle of light
for a miracle of life.

The family gathers round the bed.
Water on the boil, the kettle smoking steam.
Sundown.
We light the fifth candle of Chanukah.

Baruch atah Adonai,
Elohaynu Melech Ha'Olam,
Asher kidyshanu b'mitsvo-tov
V'etzy-vanu, l'had lik nair,
Shel Chanukah.

The candle is lit and burning bright,
a child is born unto the night.
He does not cry nor sing aloud,
his pale blue eyes with destiny endowed.
His supple skin already holds
the scars of a life yet to unfold.

His triumphant arrival into a changing world,
a life before our eyes unfurled.
Though challenges before him soon await,
the hands that hold him are hands of fate.
When the candles have melted
and their flames flickered out,
the sixth candle of Chanukah will burn, no doubt.

And so will the seventh as will the eighth,
for eighty-nine years through love and through faith.
The days will pass quickly, so will the years,
good times, bad times, laughter and tears.
Come let us celebrate this wondrous night,
as the fifth candle of Chanukah burns ever so bright.

My Pavlysh

In a hollow valley.
On hallowed soil.
In a little stone house
swept neat and tidy by a little straw broom,
a baby is born in my Pavlysh.

Restless birds
sing at the dawn of life.
A child,
sucks in vain on a crust of bread,
on his mother's withered bosom.

Dust rises from the earth,
in my Pavlysh.
Old men take the sun, smoking what they've rolled.
Tired women hang themselves out on the lines.
This, too, is my Pavlysh.

In my Pavlysh people sing and people dance.
There is dirt on the old men's shoes.
The women laugh so hard, so hard they cry.
Everyone stinks of celebration —
in my Pavlysh.

And sons of fathers go off to big cities.
They go off and they never return.
Sons of mothers who shall win great bounties.
But the fathers know what the mothers know not —
their sons will never return to their Pavlysh.

An old man dies beside a dung heap,
an old man, a pious man,
on his way to a better place.
No cold dwellings, no damp shirt or fraying talis.
His body will freeze with the night and thaw with the dawn.
There is death, too, in my Pavlysh.

But with every death comes a new life,
and a baby is born in my Pavlysh.
And like the restless birds
that sing at the dawn of life,
a baby sings out in the silence of a new day.

And when he is grown to be a fine man,
a fine man of Pavlysh he will be.
He will leave the place where he was born,
he will go forth out into the world with his dreams,
and he will remember
my Pavlysh.

The Road To Krasilov

On the road to another town.
One hoof beat—two.
A rattling cart shakes bags of grain.

On a dusty road to another town.
The next town,
and the next town—
the next town after that.
Try to persuade the sun to shine but one more
lonely hour.

The road to Krasilov.
Dark in day as is at night.
Wily crows watch every move,
they await even a modest spill.
An old oak tells lies to the wind.
How could its branches bend any lower?

"Where do you take your grain today, young man?"
"To Krasilov," the young man tells the tree.
"To see that young girl again?"
"I could easily earn more in Kiev," replies the young man.
"Yes, I suppose you very well could."

Another lonely mile and another lonely sunset.
Day escapes beneath an elastic horizon.
The young man has been fooled again.
But his purpose is clear, his will intact.
He will endure the shameless elements:
the biting wind, the stony ground,
and the raindrops,
falling hard like needles that pierce his supple skin.

He carries on upon the road to Krasilov.
To sell his grain and to pick his flower—
a budding rose.
Thunderburst awakens him from a restless daydream.
The crows have stolen his grain but love awaits him still,
on the road to Krasilov.

The Grain Merchant

From shtetl to shtetl.
The grain merchant
bag in hand
packs a little case
collects a few old marigolds
has a sip of whiskey
sweet taste on his tongue.

The grain merchant.
Sets off on his daily journey
sometimes takes a week
often takes its toll
collects a little money
has a sip of whiskey
bitter taste on his tongue.

The grain merchant comes into town.
Weary and tired and hungry
grain to sell
stories to tell
collects a few new clients
a toast of whiskey—
l'chaim!, l'chaim!

So the grain merchant sets out for home.
Weary and tired and hungry
his family awaits him
with anticipation
for he's collected a little money.
So they boast and they toast a taste of whiskey
sweet taste on the tongue
of the grain merchant.

The Dung Heap

He dare not breathe,
the young man beneath the dung heap.
Footsteps draw near.
Soldiers ready long, smoky rifles.
Noxious vapors squeeze swollen temples like a
python grips its prey.

A muffled sound screams out.
Something jerks wild beneath the dung heap.
An inner quake sends an invisible jolt
to the surface of his skin.
The dung heap atop of him rumbles like a volcano
about to burst, spewing its hot filling,
its red, acidic excrement flows.
Cascades of sweat and saliva gush from bloated wells.
Night falls and the young man sleeps
beneath the dung heap.

Morning comes.
The dew sleeps cool upon the dung heap.
Blood clotted dry, crusted on broken skin.
The young man, nostrils burdened by the residue,
awakens and pushes his swollen finger through the
soggy mound until it touches the cold morning air.

He slowly moves his head and plunges his lips into
the small hole he has made.
He swallows the air.
He kneads his way from the grasp of the
womb-like dregs that births him anew and
spits him out onto the cold, wet ground.

A warm hand touches his thawing arm
but he is not frightened.
It is Moshe, a familiar and trusted friend,
his touch as warm as a chick's downy fleece.
The soldiers have gone, there is work to be done;
bodies to bury and tears to be dried,
beside the dung heap.

Scars

Scars.
Have been seen.
Though not too often.
By uncle: the one upon his back.
By me: the one upon his hand.
Flesh that never healed,
that bled for days,
unattended.

Scars.
Open wounds mended by earth and prayer.
Ripped flesh torn open by unmerciful shrapnel.
Skin, parted, vulnerable to contamination.
He looked at the wound,
saw blood bubbling from the void like a tiny volcano.
He shook the blood from his hand to free his mind of the illusion.
But the vision remained clear.
Blood streamed a lake of fear.
And tears fell—tears that were happy to fall—
happy to flow from living, seeing eyes.

Scars.
Like narrow rivers of elongated flesh.
Raised mounds of crippled skin.
A ridge of oil paint on a canvas of supple dermis.
A sealed fissure, a broken promise mended.
Try and smooth them, flatten them out upon
the fragile landscape damaged by madness and war.
And now the winds won't burn anymore and the tears won't sting.
Gun shots won't ring out in the night.
Flesh binding flesh upon nature's repair of flawed restoration.

Scars?
Like tiny reminders left upon his body for remembrance eternal.
A permanent diary that never lies for it never could.
A portrait that will never fade in the sunlight.
A truth that can never be questioned.

A reality of what once was and what might have been.
A poem, a novel, a song—a story told in just one line
of superfluous, pale skin.
No need to know how the story ends, or the painful details.
Not curious about the circumstances or the meanings within.
And where are those scars now?
Buried with his memory
deep within my soul.

The Marriage of Yehoshua and Razel

A handsome couple.
Yehoshua and Razel.
The shtetl swells with pride.
Mama Fegeh and papa Moshe make final preparations.
Young girls run from house to house to collect needed things.
Even grey clouds make way for festive rays of sun.
Mandlbroyt and honey cakes bake themselves extra sweet.
It is, of course, the sweetest of all occasions.

The rebbe is late.
His carriage null by the roadside.
He rides his old mare bareback the rest of the way.
He has memorized his bruchas, penned a magniloquent sermon —
the shtetl will stand still in awe as he proclaims a union under God.
The rebbe arrives, is hurried inside.
He brushes the road from his suit, rinses clean his black face.
His white talis looks like a floating angel as it is removed from
its filthy bag.

The ceremonies commence.
Premature tears fall from wrinkled eyes
that have known too much suffering and yet
still can cry sweet water.
Yehoshua is nervous — more than he thought he would be.
He wants everything should go just right.
He remembers Abraham Nathanson's wedding.
Such meshugaas!
All the screaming children, the machetunim bickering —
Yehoshua wants a nice wedding.

The bride and groom beneath the khupe stand.
The rebbe puffs his chest out, puts his shoulders back, stands erect.
He has mastered his craft —
a perfect blend of sincere sentiment and pure shmalts.
Indeed it will be a most beautiful wedding.

The ritual completed, the ketubah endorsed.
A modest kiss and a hand for life.
Mazl-tov.
Your love should last a lifetime.

First Born

Part One: Razel's Poem

Married life,
husband, wife.
Clothes on the line,
skinny chickens boil as they
sip cherry wine.

The summer brings a baby,
linen clean and white.
The first born child,
a baby girl,
cries sofly in the night.

Baby Manya, first teeth, first steps,
precious eyes so true.
The most precious gift that God has given,
a baby girl for you.

Sheyneh Manyaleh, the rebbe comes to name you and
to say his bruchas.
The celebration soon begins,
for luck everyone pinches your tuchas!

A parent's pride in creating life
is equalled by their joy.
They have made a girl, a beautiful girl,
soon they'll be blessed with a handsome boy.

At night when all is quiet and still
and baby is sound asleep.
Razel and Yehoshua lie awake in their bed
and pray God for their Manya to keep.

Part Two: Yehoshua's Poem

How does it feel to hold a life in your arms?
A life you helped to create.
Look deep into her eyes, Yehoshua, for they are your eyes —
deep and blue and serene and shtark.
Hold her tiny hand in your big hand —
the earth holding the moon in its safe orbit.

Touch her soft face with yours,
unshaven and rough.
So fatherly.
So proud.
Kiss the layers of her neck as
she sleeps a dream upon your moving chest.

What do you feel when you feel her
soft hair upon your lips?
Or hear her soft noises and giggles?
What is it like to hold life so very dear?
The life of your first born child.
Yehoshua, you're a papa now.

Warsaw

Time to escape the brutality of the modern age.
Time to seek safe haven and new fortunes.
Time to be free from persecution, free from evil,
free from hostile warriors;
free from a life that wasn't a life.

Take a road, any road.
Where will this road lead?
Through village and valley,
through hardship and suffering—
to freedom and salvation.

To Warsaw.
Where new tomorrows await.
New possibilities, new opportunities—
a better life awaits.
Nobody searching, no one in fear—
freedom awaits.

A journey of days with nights eternal.
Stale tea leaves brew in charred cookery.
A journey of freedom but for a price.
Where will this road to freedom begin?
Where will it lead us and where will it end?

In Warsaw.
Where the streets move.
Where vendors and thieves crowd busy squares.
Where tongues fly—rapidfire.
Tongues that have well tasted freedom.
Take a taste—rejoice in the sweetness of freedom.

Settle in to a small, dark flat in Warsaw.
Arrange your papers and documentation.
You have become a citizen.
You have become Owsiej Usiatynski.
You have rights and freedom and civil obligations.
But this is only temporary,
real freedom awaits.

So you've heard about America.
The land of opportunity and outstretched arms.
Where a handshake can lead to fortune.
Where a landsman, even though a stranger,
is brother and a friend—
in America.

So we leave you now our cold and friendly Warsaw.
We thank you for your sanctuary and for giving us a son.
Now we must move on, our staid and somber Warsaw.
Our destiny awaits us upon a faraway shore.
Don't look for us again tomorrow, Warsaw—
we'll come again no more.

Four Hundred Hours

Thirty hours.
On a ship of steel, steam, and hope.
Wind and salty spray toss the vessel.
The cargo, human lives
drawn toward new frontiers.

Fifty hours.
An old man dies in triumph —
at least he has fulfilled a part of his dream,
more than most.
His family will carry on his name and his hopes.

Eighty hours.
Brittle bones creak in the sea breeze.
The bread is stale, but the whiskey still tastes sweet.
Gulls, curious passersby, rest a while upon the frowning bow.

One hundred hours.
A celebration in the cloudy night sky.
Singing and laughter, drenched in gaiety.
The laughter turns to tears — but tears of jubilation —
drenched soaken wet in gaiety.

One hundred and fifty hours.
The baby has caught a cold.
He is already a troublemaker, little Jakie.
Give him a drop of whiskey on his tongue,
he'll sleep the night away.

Two hundred hours.
It is an endless journey.
Perhaps it is really death — bittersweet, eternal.
Mouths salty dry, tempers flare — but only when strength allows.

Two hundred and fifty hours.
Pale faces pleading to heaven and God for redemption.
Let the waters part and bring us land once more.
Let the heavens comfort us in soft white down.

Three hundred hours.
Silence drifts upon the sea like a baby's whisper.
Melancholy waves toss—though reluctantly—
as if only to obey nature's behest.

Three hundred and fifty hours.
The once strong reduced to grievous despair.
Faces stare into other faces, each one pities the other more.
How the human condition prevails is a mystery.
How we've survived this far is far beyond reason.
If only for faith we shall survive another day.

Four hundred hours.
Cheers cry out in the night.
Those who found refuge in turbulent dreams awaken
to share in the jollity of the moment.
A thousand voices jubilant, rejoice.
Land is near, the journey a distant memory.
The ship's whistle blows as land draws nearer.
There are cases to prepare, combing and washing
and wellwishing.
Four hundred hours gone.
A little taste of hell for a larger taste of heaven.
May God bless us all when the four hundred hours have passed.

Elli∂ I∂lan∂

Disembarkation.
Ellis Island.
New York City.
America.
Processed.
Checked over.
Lungs.
Teeth.
Eyes.
Inoculated.
Poked.
Prodded.   Ellis Island.
Name changed.
New identity.
New world.
New opportunities.   Ellis Island.
Family.
Friends.
Freedom.
Money.
Dreams.
Hope.
America.   Ellis Island.
Prosperity.
All things new.   Ellis Island.
Port of entry.
Stamp the passport.
Immigrant status.
Uncertainties.
The future.
Awaits?

Mayn Zunim

(My Sons)

Settled into America.
Working regular.
Long, hard days earning hard money paid by the piece.
Chicago town.
Stony roads and dirty rain
stain little boys' clothes as they play in the yard.
Jakie and Alec.
Mayn Zunim.
Watching their child games.
Like boys they play.
Knee pants and smiling faces,
milk moustaches and chocolate teeth.
Help mama with the table.
Put the napkin down, then two spoons —
one for borsht, one for tea.
Such good boys, mayn zunim.
Time for school and time for friends and learning.
Don't come home too late, mayn zunim.
Sleep, sleep you mischievous boys — shluf, mayn zunim.
Wake up boys it is time for shul.
Wash your face and make your beds.
Put your best suit, it's Shabbos, mayn zunim.

Jake, Jake, the trouble you make!
Threw a stone through the neighbor's window.
Glass shatters, Mrs. Perlstein screams —
"Jakie, I'm going to pull your hair one of these days."
Jakie hides his face and mocks:
"Jakie, I'm going to pull your hair one of these days!"
Razel makes a stern face, Jakie bows his head low.
Razel swats him good on the tuchas as he waddles past.
Jakie runs, giggling, through the house and into his room.

Alec.
Mayn Alekel.
So quiet.
Papa's good boy.

32

Sits on papa's knee tickling papa's moustache.
Listens to the radio so fixed with purpose.
Swallows every sound.
A curious boy.
Wonders things.
His eyes always focused on motion, on stillness.
Plays nice games with nice boys and nice girls.
Shares his mandlbroyt with Sammy Soroka.

And how I watched mayn zunim grow.
From small, fragile boys—yinglekh—
to young men in tapered suits with fine hands.
And such things do mayn zunim know,
about the world and of life and of fascinating things.
Mayn zunim, how proud you make me.
How proud any father would be to have zunim
like mayn zunim.

The West Side

I never saw bricks standing so tall one on top of the other.
Buildings edging up skyward.
I wonder if bricks standing so tall could reach the sky.
How could people live up so high?
And walk up three flights of stairs? Vey iz mir!

I never saw streets stretch so wide, so long.
Where could these streets lead?
I wonder if streets could stretch so long they would lead to Zion.
How could someone walk down such long and endless streets?
Walking miles and miles — Vey iz mir! — such streets.

And I never saw grass so green and tall,
or flowers so yellow,
or a blue sky so very blue as this blue sky.
And here I make my family a home.
On the west side.

14th Street, Keeler, Tripp, Kildare, Karlov, Kostner,
12th Street, Grenshaw, Roosevelt Road, 15th Street,
16th Street, 22nd Street — Vey iz mir! —
Independence Boulevard, Douglas Boulevard,
The Russian Shul, Turovitz Grocery,
Zimbler's (they had everything there!),
Zweig's, Perlman's, Cohn's Shoes,
Segal Shoes — Vey iz mir! —
The Lawndale Theatre, The Central Park,
The Gold, The Marbro, The Paradise,
Horwich Bakery, Carl's, Fluky's,
The Liberty Bank,
Silversteins —
Vey iz mir! — such a place.

The west side.
Where Ben Gurion spoke at a parade outside Pinsky Hebrew Shul.
Little Tibie presented him with a bouquet of flowers.

The west side.
Where life was sunlit, clean, and everything was new and
everyone was young.

Where you knew who your friends were;
you knew who your family was;
you knew your kids' friends' names;
you knew that time was precious, that life was for living.

On the west side.
Where you could sleep in Garfield Park on a hot
summer night and the only thing that would bother you were the
mosquitoes and the yenties kvetching.
But even that was okay,
on the west side.

Where you said good morning to your neighbor,
where you knew your neighbor's business —
even if it wasn't your business.
Where you went to shul on Saturday morning.
When you actually had Shabbos clothes.
And when you stayed after services not just for the honey cake
and whiskey, but to greet your friends and wish them well,
on the west side.

Where you made your home,
where you settled down.
Where you raised your family.
Where you lived a life unlike any life.
Where you dreamed dreams unlike any dreams of old.

And where you could walk down streets so long and wide,
see buildings so high you thought they reached the sky.
Where you paved your own streets with golden dreams,
built your own skyscrapers with tall ideals.
Where you spent your days, your nights and your holy festivals.

Where you saw your visions of yesterday
transformed into dreams of today
and hopes for tomorrow.
Where the limits of success had no boundaries, no frontiers,

for success was limitless, for failure was unknown, unthinkable.
Where life was good, wholesome, and innocent.
Like never before.
Like never again.
On the west side.

The Installment Dealer

House to house he travelled.
The installment dealer.
Wearing shoe leather down to the cobblestone.
On his route he challenged the seasons.
He appeared on your front porch,
he was known for he came well recommended.
He was invited in.
Offered tea and coffee cakes.
He sat in the best chair.
He came with samples from Gilbert Drapery.
Not the most beautiful or the most expensive,
but what his clients could have easily afforded.
Whatever he brought was good enough,
who knew any better?

Mrs. Walenski made her selections.
The installment dealer reached for his payment book.
Five dollars now and a dollar a week.
Mrs. Walenski's head fell almost to the floor,
her large eyes fixed upon the payment book,
then shifted slowly to the installment dealer.
"Mister Satin," she said as she held out her large hands.
"Have another piece of coffee cake, I made it myself."
"I'll take what you can give me," said the installment dealer
as he set his tea cup down and reached into his jacket
for his pencil.
"You'll give me more next time," he said as he took a bite of
coffee cake, crumbs falling to his lap that he brushed to the floor.

The installment dealer arrived at his next appointment.
To the south side to visit an Italian family.
He entered an empty flat.
Was greeted by skinny children and a fat woman who hugged him
so close he nearly disappeared into her bosom.
It is another poor family story.
They have just arrived and haven't a cent.
"I'll take what you can give me," said the installment dealer.
"You'll give me what you can next time."

The Italian woman embraced him;
his frail frame disappeared again into her bosom.
The children laughed out loud.
"I'll pick you up on Wednesday morning at nine.
We'll go see Gladman.
You'll have the most beautiful furniture on the south side."

The installment dealer sold everything.
You name it, he sold it.
He bought by Pritikin, by Midwest.
On Halsted, on Jefferson Boulevard.
Furniture, clothing, any household necessity.
And what a talker.
At three times the price he could sell a shmate to a princess
or a castle to a pauper.
He was a household name.
Like a part of the family.
Invited to all the gentile simchas —
weddings, communions.

Was there at the baptism of Esposito the Italian's son,
at the funeral of Wisnewski's cousin.
He was there when you needed him,
when you didn't have a dime.
The installment dealer.
The customer peddler.
With his payment book, his installment plan, his samples,
and his kind heart.
He took care of business that your family
should have what it needed,
that his family should have
what it needed.

Razel, A Rose

(For Rose Satin)

A woman I never knew
for she lived not long enough to have known me in this
life.
She was my zayde's reddest rose,
she was his faithful and loving wife.

They shared together the truest love
bound not by legal ties.
But bound by sanctity and respect,
and the beauty in her eyes.

She was as strong as the strongest bridge,
gentle as an autumn breeze.
Her soothing voice, her placid touch,
could calm the raging seas.

Intimidated not by modern things,
by progress fast or slow.
And by any device for a pizza slice,
she always went with the flow.

Though held traditions close at heart,
she lived in the present tense.
Her family came first and foremost,
with love, concern, and reverence.

When bubbe Razel died, I have been told,
zayde's heart it nearly froze.
'Till her memory thawed and softened it again,
like the petals of a beautiful rose.

Dr. Max Dolnick

Dr. Dolnick was a quiet man.
A bespectacled and thin man, of frail health.
A close friend of my zayde.
Eloquent, scholarly.
An active Zionist.
Recruited zayde
to be an active Zionist.
Dr. Max Dolnick.
A good friend, an intimate friend.
They never dined, never socialized.
Embraced ideas and loyalty—respect—
but never each other.
Not a rich man, Dr. Dolnick.
Gave money to his patients who
could not afford their prescriptions.
He did not drive.
Zayde would occasionally drive him in his '41 Nash
to see his patients.
And zayde smoked too much—back then.
Dr. Dolnick said "Sam, quit smoking now and you'll live
another forty years."
Zayde quit smoking.
And lived another forty years.

I remember the portrait of Dr. Dolnick
hanging from the landing
at the Dr. Max Dolnick Community Center.
It was the first thing you saw
as you came in through the front door.
A portrait of a man with a hollow face—
a wooden face—seemingly—with small, round glasses
circling small round eyes.

So there I was one day,
skimming the pages of the telephone directory.
Looking for a namesake,
a relative—
a landsman.

Someone who could tell me more about Dr. Dolnick.
Someone who could bear witness to the man,
his existence,
his friendship with my zayde.
Any detail:
A photograph.
A memoir.
A faint recollection.
A story—made up or not—
something to inspirit the myth.
Something to confirm that there was
a man who I knew not
who meant so much to a man I knew so well.
Whose car I drove,
whose bed I slept,
whose hand I touched.
The same hand that outstretched and greeted
Dr. Max Dolnick.

And as for me, I never saw the man
but for his portrait hanging.
Often had I touched the hand that had
often touched his.
I never heard him speak though I have heard
others speak of him.
He was a friend of my zayde's—
a dear friend, a close friend.
And one day—maybe—
when our spirits together will be,
will Dr. Max Dolnick be a friend to me.

The L.Z.A.

The Labor Zionist Alliance.
Farband Chapter.
Working for the new homeland.
Palestine.
Israel.
The land of our forefathers —
our people.

Meetings take place,
ideas for raising money —
raising consciousness.
Raising the understanding of how important it was
for the Jewish people to have a land of their own.
A place — a special place —
to call home,
to call their very own.

All the meetings.
All the stained black-bottomed coffee cups and
smoldering cigarette butts in square glass ashtrays —
they really smoked back then — cigars, too.
And they drank coffee, and nobody knew from cappuccino or
Sweet and Low.
They called the meeting to order by pounding a gavel —
a real wooden gavel —
I saw it once in zayde's top drawer.

And the work continued.
Work for the homeland.
The Labor Zionist Alliance.
The workers,
the backbone.
The heart and soul,
the toil and tears of a young and growing nation.

The United Pavolotcher's Society

How alike we are to the seeds of trees that plant their roots
so deep into the ground.
We, whose roots share a common tree,
planted deep beneath a common soil.

How alike are we to clouds that spread their shadows
far across the landscape.
Clouds that rain heavy rain and soak our common soil,
drench our common roots, and sprout our common seed.

We, who are the scion of a past life,
a past land,
uprooted and transplanted like trees,
trees that survived the cyclones and the torrents,
the passages of time and (r)evolution;
dusk and dawn,
days and nights
of prayers and psalms,

that one day we will be reunited in our land,
our home,
our Pavlyshes,
our Krasilovs.
Beneath the ground,
upon the ground,
and far reaching to the sky.
We will drink sweet wine from Elijah's cup
and we shall sing Dayenu.

This is our brotherhood,
our sisterhood.
Our resting place in a land
far from the land of our fathers.
But it is only a temporary one.
We have paid our dollar for our plots of land.
We await the day to answer God's calling.
When we will awake to a new and brighter sunrise.
When we will walk once more along dusty roads.
When we will smile upon our neighbors,
and raise our voices high,
high above the wailing call of the shofar
that will sound freedom,
redemption, and salvation.
We will be reunited with our land and our people,
with our God Almighty who will bring us forth once again from
bondage and deliver us to our promised land.
And though it may not be Zion it is *our* Zion.
The land of our fathers.
The land of our home.
For today,
tomorrow,
and for all eternity.

Maplewood

There is a modest three flat on Maplewood Street
where my family used to live.
And I lived there, too, as a little boy.
And during the great migrations
from the west side to the north,
to a newer, better, safer place to live,
came my family to Maplewood Street.
They came with old furniture and new hopes,
strong traditions and happy hearts,
joyful hearts.

Bubbe and zayde slept in the back bedroom
that overlooked the yard, garage, and alley.
Grama and grampa had the smaller bedroom,
shaded by the Zanin's building next door.
Mom and aunt Phyllis slept on the back porch
that was converted into a girl's room.
How carefree the times —
how innocent, how tranquil.
Breakfast on the round kitchen table
that eventually became mine and since discarded.
Lunch on the job or at school or at a friend's house.
Dinner on the table at the same time every night.
Everyone had their own place at the table on Maplewood Street.
And if someone liked their vegetable soup strained,
or the skin taken off their cold chicken polkies they didn't have to ask.
If someone spilled their ginger ale or left crumbs of challah on the table
it didn't matter and no one became angry.

At home on Maplewood Street.
Where your friends were made to feel like family
and your family felt like friends.
Where the door was always open and the fridge was always full;
the laughter always hearty and warmth and love
a comfort to anyone who sought it.

We walked up three flights of stairs to get home
on Maplewood Street.
Zayde would take one stair at a time.
Sometimes he would stop and rest on the landing between floors.
He would look out of the window with his hand resting
upon the polished banister.
On Maplewood Street there was a mezuzah on every door post;
a clanking in every radiator;
a fake fireplace in the front room that might have been real once
but no one knew for sure.

There was a little table and stool in the front hall
where the telephone was.
The phone was black and you dialed with your finger or a pencil.
Zayde would dial one number at a time, slowly.
He would look at the first number, insert his finger in the dial and
spin it round hard.
Then the second, the third, and so forth.
Sometimes he would place the handset down
until he had finish dialing.
Then he would slowly lift it up and press it hard to his ear.

And Maplewood was where family was.
Maplewood *was* family.
Maplewood was where the Blechman Cousin's Club met
to play cards and talk and drink schnapps.
Where zayde argued about uncle Moysh smoking in the house.
Zayde thought that since *he* quit smoking *everyone* should
quit smoking.
On Maplewood.
Where Jakie came to spend a few days to recover from some very
personal surgery that left him sitting on an inflatable bagel.
Maplewood.
Where Phyllis and Art came to sleep and to weep
the night little Shari died.
Where on Wednesday bubbe would come home from downtown
with her pretty little hat, her white gloves,
from returning what she bought at Mandel Brothers on Monday.

Where friends would come to play kayoodle.
Where lovers kissed their first kiss outside the front door.
(Even my first kiss was there outside the front door on Maplewood.)

Maplewood.
The only home I ever knew that was a home.
Where I was a child.
Where my zayde lived.
Where Friday night we all ate together.
Where we watched Ed Sullivan in the front room on Sunday nights.
Where I played Tarzan and even had a rubber Tarzan knife.

When zayde would come home late on a Saturday night
I would lie awake in my bed listening for the sound
of the car door slamming then zayde walking slowly
up the stairs and in the door.
I would wait until he took out his teeth and pulled the covers
over his head.
He would fall asleep so quickly and begin to snore.
The sound of zayde snoring put me fast to sleep.

Maplewood.
Where I got the chicken pox and wet the bed.
Where Lucky gave me my first (and only) black eye.
Where some bullies punctured my first basketball,
(even though it wasn't a real one).
Where I waited outside in my little baseball uniform for
someone to pick me up.
Someone who never did.

Maplewood.
Where I was afraid to go into the basement alone.
Where I thought I heard witches laughing on the back porch.
Where jesters chased me in my dreams.
Where zayde let me come into his bed.
Where I had my first giraffe.
Where the Hofmanns were our neighbors.
Mrs. Hart, the landlady.
David Mason, the only boy who invited me over.

Mr. Schick who fixed television sets.
The O'Brians and Haleys who would greet you from their yard.

Maplewood.
The street where I lived—
once—
as a boy.
Where I can still feel zayde's beard scratching
my face as I lay beside him on his bed.
Where I can still smell his after shave,
and hear him scraping his burnt challah over the sink,
and sipping his tea from the saucer,
and cursing every other driver,
and leaving home for the last time...
on Maplewood.

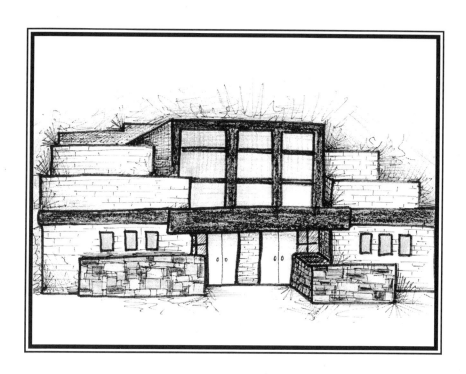

The Center

Where did zayde go every morning?
Every afternoon?
Every night?
What was his business?
His doings?
His occupation?

He founded a community center on California Avenue.
Named it after his beloved friend Dr. Max Dolnick.
The Center was his life —
the very *center* of his life.
There from morning till night
making necessary plans and
arrangements.
Looking after everything that required looking after.

I remember the red calendar book that he kept
inside of the right top drawer,
or sometimes left open upon his desk.
Every day a different function.
Meetings, luncheons, affairs, dinners,
banquets, rummage sales, bazaars,
and of course the High Holiday services —
that was the most important event of the year.
How he would haggle with Cantor Lind over his salary.
But zayde would always get his way.
Cantor Lind was worth twice what he was paid
and would have worked for half of that.
He told me on the phone one day how he loved my zayde,
how he embraced him and how he had even kissed him once.

There were many special people at the Center.
Hymie Drucker, uncle Art's father,
worked nights and smoked in the bathroom.
He only took a puff or two before putting the cigarette
out between his fingers and stashed it behind his ear
for later.

Eleanora Wilson was the first black person I ever saw.
She worked for my zayde.

She called him Mister Satin.
That seems odd to me now.
And did they fight.
Zayde must have fired her a thousand times.
Eleanora took care of me when I was young,
just like she took care of zayde as he got older.
One afternoon she sat me down at the large
wooden table in the kitchen at the Center.
I must have been around five years old and the Cub's game
was on an old television with a coat hanger antenna.
She asked me if I wanted something special.
(Of course I did.)
She cut a square slice of vanilla ice cream from the carton
and dropped it into a bowl.
She took out a bottle of Coke from the fridge.
She poured the Coke on top of the ice cream,
gave me a spoon and set the bowl down in front of me.
"Your grandad likes these," she said.
It was my first Coke float.
I still remember Eleanora every time I have one.

Eleanora had many children —
nieces, nephews, in-laws —
who would come to work at the Center on special occasions,
especially during the big Pioneer Women bazaar.
A.J., her son-in-law,
was the first person to let me go into the boiler room,
(because zayde never let me).
Wilma-Jean, Eleanora's daughter, was very beautiful.
She would work in the coat check during the bazaar.
Another daughter, Bertha, would work
in the kitchen with Eleanor.
Her children found her dead one morning in her bed.
They said that something burst in her brain.
But she wasn't the first — or the last —
of Eleanora's children to die
so very young.

So many memories of the Center.
Of zayde behind his desk,
arguing with someone on the telephone,
locking the doors at night to go home,
shaking both doors extra hard to make sure they were locked.
I would often come and have lunch with zayde at the Center from
my grammar school just across the street.
We would sit in his office and eat together,
or go to Robby's where zayde would have mushroom barley soup.
"Give me the barley and keep the mushrooms," he used to say.
He would eat chicken or a cheese sandwich—muenster—
and a baked apple or rice pudding for dessert
that he would drown in half and half.

And the Center had a leaky roof that always resisted mending.
Zayde was always worried about that roof.
I loved to sit in zayde's chair behind his big desk and look through
the pages of his date book.
I was a child and never worried about leaky roofs or date books.
In the end the leaky roof always wins.
So fold the tables, stack up the chairs and return the table linen.
Pack up the files and lock up all the doors.
(Shake them extra good and hard.)
Say good bye to the past and
remember how good it was.
Pick up the phone just one more time and dial SHeldrake 3–4398.
The number has been disconnected but there is still a voice
on the other end of the line.
It's Mr. Satin calling from the Dolnick Center.
I'll take that call.

Friends and Rivals

Friends and rivals filled zayde's life:
with joy,
with laughter,
aggravation and strife.

Mr. Fink and zayde would constantly fight,
it didn't matter who was wrong or right.
It could have been cloudy and one would say bright,
it could have been daytime, the other would say night.

With Katz it was a difference of opinions and views,
about politics, religion, Israel, and Jews.
About who blew the shofar on Yom Kippur eve,
and how much the bluzer in turn would receive.

With Max Clar there was laughter and friendship replete,
with Pinsky rapport though impetus to compete.
With Stein due respect, with Patt nothing less,
with Fannie Poster agitation, but handled with finesse.

Though in times of commotion and subtle disarray,
zayde somehow managed to always get his way.
If he hollered or screamed it was not to offend,
for he loved and respected both rival and friend.

The Shvits

On Roosevelt Road.
Take a shvits, trim, and massage.
Such a mekhaye.

"Feh"

"Feh," zayde would say,
as he gave a little grepts.
Always made me laugh.

False Teeth

Sometimes falling out.
Put them in a cup at night.
I tried them on once.

Pants Over Pajamas

Just like Dick Van Dyke.
Pants over his pajamas.
In time for supper.

Tea

Sugar cube in mouth.
Spill hot tea on the saucer.
Take a slurp or two.

Chaver Satin

(Recollections of Friends)

A friend to all.
To those who knew him from the Center,
those who knew him from shul.
Those who knew him as a neighbor,
those who knew as I knew him.

A chaver is a friend,
who is there when you need a friend.
Chaver Satin was there when you needed a friend.
Chaver Satin was there when you needed a favor,
especially to book a room with short notice.
He would always manage to squeeze you in somehow.

Chaver Satin would make sure you had what you needed.
That the coffee was set up and the tablecloths were clean.
And if you asked for a donation,
Chaver Satin would write you a check —
maybe it was a small check —
but you could always count on Chaver Satin.

And Chaver Satin was stubborn.
And Chaver Satin always had to have things done his way.
But it was always for the best.
And Chaver Satin — no matter how stubborn —
was always fair.

There aren't many people left in the world
like Chaver Satin,
true and dedicated friends.
Whose words are worth their weight in gold,
who you can call at anytime if you need to.
But then again,
there never were many people in the world like Chaver Satin.

Prelude To Waldheim

I was only fifteen.
I had my learner's permit.
Zayde would pick me up at home on Washtenaw.
He would move over and slide back the front seat.
The long drive to the cemetery was getting too much for him,
and seeing how I could drive —
and was a good driver,
(even at fifteen),
everyone felt better about zayde not driving so far.

I knew the way to the cemetery.
I had gone with zayde so many times before.
California to Lawrence.
Right on Lawrence to Manor —
left turn,
cross the train tracks,
continue south to Irving Park.
Turn left on Harlem until you arrive
at the front gate of Jewish Waldheim Cemetery.

First we would stop at the office and zayde would
go inside and take care of business.
I would turn on the radio while he was inside —
he wouldn't let me play it when we were driving.
Zayde returned and we would drive to where the
family plot was.
He would survey the graves:
bubbe's,
little Shari's,
his friends',
his own.

I liked looking at the pictures on the head stones.
Sometimes you had to lift a metal cover to see the picture,
sometimes they were locked —
like bubbe's.

Zayde would tell me not to walk on the people.
Zayde would pick up twigs and fallen leaves from
around bubbe's grave.
He would walk, row by row, making mental notes
of any problems—weeds, chips in the head stones,
grass that needed cutting.
We would stop at the office once more before we
left so zayde could report any problems.

We would leave the cemetery and go for a bite.
We wouldn't talk on the way home.
Occasionally zayde would comment
about my driving,
that I was going too fast or too slow.
But he was diplomatic about it.

He would drop me off at home and slide over behind the wheel.
He would push the seat up and re-adjust the mirrors.
He thanked me for taking him and then drove off.
Sometimes I would kiss him good bye.
I would wait until he crossed Devon Avenue before going inside.
I would often wonder how many more times I would drive
zayde to the cemetery.

Yellow Jaundice

I took zayde to the doctor for a check up before his
annual pilgrimage to uncle Al's for the winter.
I waited outside for a long time in a corridor at Edgewater Hospital.
Zayde came out, was silent.
He said he would have to be admitted at once.
He wasn't going to be able to go to California,
not now, anyway.

The doctor said it was jaundice.
His skin was yellow,
his eyes were yellow.
They would have to run tests to see what was making him yellow.
They found that he had a blockage somewhere in his stomach.
It would have to be removed.
I thought it was because he ate too much challah.

The date was arranged.
Surgery postponed because he was running a fever.
They said despite his age he was healthy enough to undergo
the operation.
They gave no prognosis.
Everyone came in from out of town.
When they opened him up they found cancer in his pancreas.
He survived the operation.
He was put into intensive care.
What a horrible place.
The man in the next bed was recovering from open-heart surgery.
He was pale and had tubes coming out from everywhere.
What a sight.

There was never any talk of recovery or of zayde going home.
Just talk of observation and getting zayde strong enough to eat.
Doctors came in and out.
Nurses, some nasty some nice,
forced ice chips and apple juice into zayde's dry mouth.

All I did was take zayde for a check-up.

I'll Take You Home Now, Zayde

There were times when I thought the best thing for zayde
was to take him home.
If he's going to recuperate why not let him recuperate in his
own bed.
If he's going to get well again why not let him get well in his
own bed.
If he's ever going to eat again why not let him his eat his
own challah, drink his own borsht,
and sip his own tea
from his own cup
in his own bed
in his own house.
And if he is going to die what better place to die than
in his own bed
in his own house.

I suggested that we take zayde home.
No one agreed.
The hospital was the best place for him.
He would have the proper care and attention.
"I'll take zayde home," I would say to myself.
"I'll give him the proper care and attention he needs."
But no one would listen to a teenage boy.
Had they, maybe zayde would have gotten well.
Had they, maybe he could have gone to California.
Had they, maybe he would have never died.
Had they...

Witness

Six months dying in a small
stinky room.
Edgewater Hospital.
Where his body shrank smaller each passing day.
A tube in his neck sustained his life
which wasn't much of a life.
It merely postponed death,
put it on hold.
He was fed through a tube,
urinated through another.
Another in his arm to make him strong.
He dirtied his sheets.
Sores and blisters on his back and legs
were constant ailments.
We tried to keep him comfortable
by rubbing him down with lotions.
Moaning and dying more every day.
Every painful movement brought him closer to the end.
He counted rabbis and salt shakers,
he recollected his bar-mitzvah,
his wedding.
Called out names of his parents and prophets,
childhood friends,
and relations.
Sang and chanted
and spoke in tongues.
But he was still my zayde.
And fascinated by it all, I observed his death.
Witnessing the passing of a life
from one realm to another.

Pesach in Acapulco

Six months of suffering.
Watching others suffering as
zayde lay,
weightless,
suffering.

I was sixteen.
Zayde's car was mine now.
It would never be his again.
I drove his car —
my car —
to Edgewater Hospital to see him everyday.
No one knew I wasn't going to school.

For six months I watched my zayde dying.
I watched my family,
coming and going,
in and out,
consultations with doctors,
decisions not being made.

Grama and grampa had a trip long planned to Israel.
"Go," we told them, "pa will be alright."
Mom and dad had a trip long planned to Hawaii.
"Go," we told them, "pa will be alright."
I was invited to Acapulco for Pesach.
"Go," they told me, "Zayde will be alright."

I went one last time to see him,
to tell him good bye and to wait for me.
He was a shadow of the zayde I had once known.
I told him, though I was sure he did not understand,
that I was going to Acapulco for Pesach.

Zayde always knew he would die on Yontev.
I was at breakfast on Saturday morning at
a kosher hotel in Acapulco, Mexico.
It was the Sabbath.
It was also Yontev.

Suddenly, I was overcome by morbid thoughts.
I ran to the phone in the corridor outside of the dining room.
I called home collect.
Mom answered.
I asked if everything was okay.
I told her I felt that something was wrong—
maybe with zayde.
She couldn't hold back that something *was* wrong,
the pauses were too long.
She told me.
Zayde died last night.
On Yontev—on Shabbos—just as he knew he would.

Everyone had just eaten dinner.
They had been to the hospital a few hours earlier.
The hospital called advising that the family should come,
it wouldn't be long before he would be gone.

I hung up the phone and returned to my breakfast.
I informed my gracious hosts that my zayde had died.
They consoled me but I did not need consolation.
I excused myself and walked out into the hot morning sun,
stopped in the circular driveway,
there was a palm tree there.
I looked up towards the sky and said aloud to God:
"please take care of my zayde."

I did not return for the funeral.
Zayde would not have wanted me there anyway.
I had done enough.
I had comforted him enough.
He had waited until I had gone away to die.
He did not want me to see him that way,
overcome by the final shadow,
wrapped in his shroud,
covered by his talis.
I hoped they had shaved him nice and combed his hair
with a wave like he liked it.

When I returned home from Acapulco
the family was still in town.
I don't know what everyone thought about me not being at
zayde's funeral.
Selfish, I would have to assume.
I wouldn't have blamed them if they had.
But zayde knew why and understood.
That was the most important thing.

I can not remember the long flight home,
it was so long ago.
Maybe it was all a dream.
Perhaps I hadn't gone to Acapulco at all.
Maybe I had invented the entire scheme.

And life went on.
I went back to school.
Was held back a year until I made up what work I had to.
And did.
I drove alone to the cemetery many times.
I talked to zayde.
I told him about my life.
I never cried until that day,
nearly a year later.
I was at Sari's house.
It suddenly occurred to me that my zayde
was no longer there.
I locked myself in the bathroom and I cried.
I remembered what we had gone through,
zayde and me.
All of those afternoons in the hospital.
All of those things we said and shared.
All of the things I had seen
that I probably should not have seen.

Zayde's soul was finally at rest inside of me.
Our lives, mine on earth and his in heaven, could go on.
Peacefully,
together,
united by our memories,
our souls,
and the love we had
and often shared,
and still,
to this day,
remains.

When Time Shattered Dreams

(1981)

Shattered dreams on the laughing porch
with one toy box,
giraffe,
and the white wicker tantrum.

Seeing and feeling one hand above my head
as the gray man sleeps besides me —
as he always does —
a child's peace of mind.
Seeing images through thread wound rings,
the mind's eye of a little boy.

Playing games on checkerboard floors.
Always trying to find turtles and birds buried in the yard.
The peeling of the false, brick-like siding.
The clothes line, and the other line.
And the little blue pool,
always waiting for the other children to come and play.

My zayde died there,
I can still hear him in my dreams.
Not calling names,
or counting rabbis,
but reaching out a thin and frail hand
through delusions in his mind.
Delusions implanted by illness and disease.

As he lay there waiting to die alone,
so did I.
The sand ran all around my feet,
the sun, scorching my skin.
The beach and the hour glass were one,
but fate was far beyond the setting sun.

Time shattered dreams once more,
while smiles turned to frowns.
Shattered dreams of a little boy
and an old man,
and a life long lived,

lived long,
lived well,
but ended,
as do all lives.
As will mine.

When will time not shatter our dreams?
When will our lives run longer than sandy beaches?
When will our childhood dreams cease to torment us and
wake us in the night?
Forever is never and never it seems
will time shatter time
instead of our dreams.

My Zayde

My zayde was an old man.
From the day I first knew him
until the day he passed away.

We shared a small bedroom
with two twin beds.
I was glad to have someone to sleep with.

He had two dressers,
one is now mine.
It is my most beloved possession.

My zayde would take his teeth out
before going to bed.
He would rinse his mouth with warm salt water in the morning.

He would eat toasted challah and drink Sanka for breakfast.
He wore thick eye glasses, a hat,
and a cardigan sweater with a shirt and tie.

He had white hair and a white moustache.
He combed his hair so it made a wave.
My hair does that now.

He used an electric razor to shave,
he'd splash on Skin Bracer
that I could taste when I kissed him.

And after I moved away I would still sleep
at zayde's on Friday nights.
We would watch *Sanford and Son* and *Chico and the Man.*

Sometimes he would let me stay up late to watch Johnny Carson.
I'd always fall asleep until I heard zayde get out of bed and say
"Johnny was good, I'll pish, take out mayn teeth, and come right to
bed."

On Saturday morning he would drop me off at home
or sometimes I would go with him to shul.
Then he would take me to Robby's for lunch.

He ate there almost every day.
All the waitresses loved him and called him Sam.
Even the cook would come out and say hello.

Zayde drove a big blue Chevy Malibu.
The seats would get so hot in the summertime.
Zayde took me to a picnic once on the south side.

My zayde was a beautiful man.
He was kind and he loved me more
than anyone.

One day I hope I will be someone's zayde.
A great-grandfather to my grandson's son.
I will tell my great-grandchildren about my zayde:

How he would sit in the yard on summer afternoons
wearing bermuda shorts, a white sleeveless undershirt,
black socks and slippers.

He would read the *Forwards*
and fall asleep on the mesh webbed chair
while I would play in the yard.

Grama would call us up for supper
and we would eat cold chicken sandwiches
on challah with mayonnaise.

My zayde reminds me of a day
just like today;
cloudy, warm, and gray.

And my zayde is still a part of me,
and now he is a part of you.
His beautiful memory enshrined in our hearts,
our minds,
and upon these pages
forever.

Obituary

SATIN

Sam (Sheika) Satin
beloved husband of the late Rose (Razel),
devoted father of Mary (Bernard) Lurie,
Jack, Alex (Shirley),
devoted zayde of Phyllis, Arthur,
Terri, Bob, David, Diane, Michael,
Jeff, Mark, Jamie, Cory,
Neil, Ricky, Ross, Tracey, and Glenn.

Founder, manager and chairman of Dr. Max A. Dolnick
Community Center,
Dr. Dolnick High Holiday Services,
President United Pavolotcher Society since 1925,
Westside Pinsky Farband Shule,
Sec'y Ben-Gurion branch Labor Zionist Alliance,
member of Bnai Jacob Congregation,
Associated Talmud Torahs,
member Friends of Pioneer Women,
member Association of Americans and Canadians in Israel,
member of Krasilover Verein,
active in Jewish National Fund,
Israel Bonds, Jewish United Fund,
member of the Northwest Home for the Aged,
Histraduth.

Loved by all who knew him.
In lieu of flowers contributions to the Pioneer Women would
be appreciated.
Services Tuesday, April 8, 1980
2 p.m. at Original Weinstein & Sons Chapel 3019 W. Peterson.
Interment United Pavolotcher Cemetery,
Jewish Waldheim.
Chapel visitation at time of services. Information 561-1890.

RICHARD MORRIS USATINSKY was born in Chicago in 1963 and was educated at DeWitt Clinton Elementary School, Stephen T. Mather High School, and DePaul University (B.F.A., M.A.), Chicago, Illinois. He has produced five original plays including *Happy Man, Eloise, The Armoire, Farewell, Mister White* (Chicago Dramatists Workshop, 1991), and *The Providence of God* (Lookmanohands Productions, 1992). Mr. Usatinsky is a member of The Dramatists Guild and The National Writers Union.

JUDITH SOL–DYESS was born in Lérida, Spain and is a student at The School of the Art Institute of Chicago. She has been an apprentice artist at the City of Chicago's Gallery 37 and has won numerous awards for artistic excellence in Chicago, and in her native Cataluña.